Dominoes

THE WRONG TROUSERS™

OXFORD
UNIVERSITY PRESS

Great Clarendon Street, Oxford OX2 6DP

Oxford University Press is a department of the University of Oxford.
It furthers the University's objective of excellence in research, scholarship, and education by publishing worldwide in

Oxford New York

Auckland Cape Town Dar es Salaam Hong Kong Karachi
Kuala Lumpur Madrid Melbourne Mexico City Nairobi
New Delhi Shanghai Taipei Toronto

With offices in

Argentina Austria Brazil Chile Czech Republic France Greece
Guatemala Hungary Italy Japan Poland Portugal Singapore
South Korea Switzerland Thailand Turkey Ukraine Vietnam

First published 2003
2008 2007 2006 2005
10 9 8 7 6 5

ISBN-13: 978 0 19 424396 4
ISBN-10: 0 19 424396 6

A complete recording of this Dominoes edition of *The Wrong Trousers*™ is available on cassette ISBN 0 19 424374 5

An English Language Teaching Video adaptation of *The Wrong Trousers*™ is available on videocassette from Oxford University Press: VHS PAL 0 19 459025 9, VHS SECAM 0 19 459026 7, NTSC 0 19 459027 5

Printed in Hong Kong

ACKNOWLEDGEMENTS

Illustrations by: Steve Cox/Peter, Fraser and Dunlop pp iv, 6, 12, 13, 18, 19, 24, 30, 31, 39, 43, 44

Dominoes

SERIES EDITORS: BILL BOWLER AND SUE PARMINTER

Text adaptation by Bill Bowler

Based on Nick Park's Oscar®-Winning Characters

LEVEL ONE ■ 400 HEADWORDS

The Dominoes edition of *The Wrong Trousers* is based on Nick Park's Oscar®-Winning Characters. Nick Park is a three-time Academy Award® winner in the category of Best Animated Short for the films *Creature Comforts*, *The Wrong Trousers* and *A Close Shave*. All three films were created at Aardman, where Nick is a Co-Director with founders Peter Lord and David Sproxton. At Aardman, Nick has also served as a director and animator on numerous projects including pop promos, title sequences and inserts for children's television.

BEFORE READING

1 In *The Wrong Trousers* you are going to read about Wallace, Gromit and the Penguin.

Who has these things in the story? What do you think? Mark them W (Wallace), G (Gromit), or P (the Penguin)

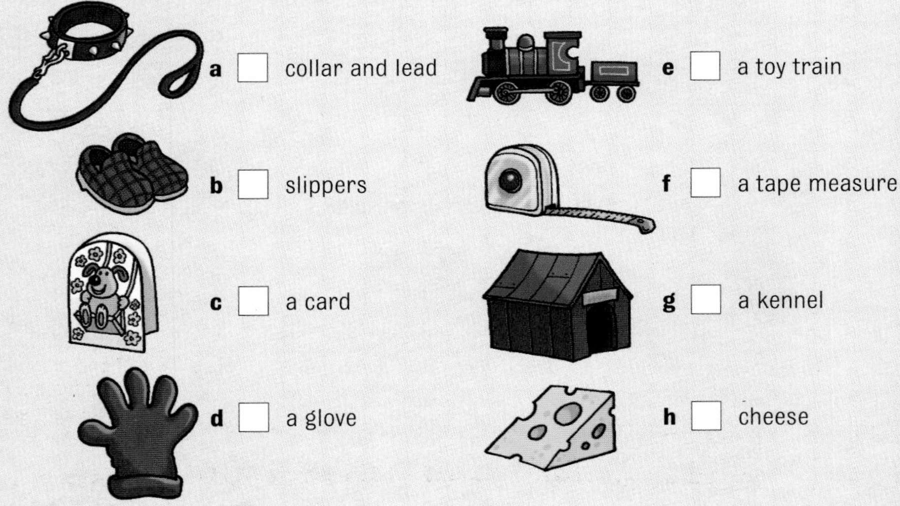

a ☐ collar and lead
b ☐ slippers
c ☐ a card
d ☐ a glove
e ☐ a toy train
f ☐ a tape measure
g ☐ a kennel
h ☐ cheese

2 Why is the story called *The Wrong Trousers*? Finish the sentence.

Because Wallace puts on different trousers one day, and he . . .

a ☐ loses all his money.
b ☐ can't remember his name.
c ☐ does bad things in his sleep.
d ☐ loses his best friend.

Happy Birthday, Chuck!

It was early in the morning on Wednesday 12th. Gromit the dog sat at the table in the **kitchen** of the little house at 62 West Wallaby Street and made breakfast. Suddenly he remembered something. He got up from the table and went to look at the **calendar** near the door. Wednesday 12th was his birthday. There it was on the calendar in blue pen – 'Gromit's **birthday**'. Gromit took a pen and put a big blue X through the number 12.

'It's my birthday today and my friend Wallace is sleeping,' he thought, and he felt **sad**. Wallace wasn't a dog. He was a man, and Gromit lived with him at 62 West Wallaby Street.

Gromit looked at his watch. It was nine o'clock. Just then he heard a noise at the front door. 'There! That's the postman!' he thought. 'Perhaps I'm going to get some birthday **cards** this morning. Let's go and see!'

kitchen the room in the house where people make things to eat

calendar a book with all the days of the year in it, often with a different month on every page

birthday the day when someone was born

sad not happy

card something that you send to someone on their birthday

There were six letters by the front door when Gromit arrived there, and he looked at all of them carefully. Most of them were letters for Wallace. Letters in brown **envelopes** asking for money. But there was one envelope – a green one – for Gromit.

With all six letters in his mouth, Gromit ran back to the kitchen. Suddenly a **toy** train **shot** out in front of him. He stopped for a minute. The train went past and then he ran on, back to the breakfast table. There were lots of different **machines** in Wallace and Gromit's house in West Wallaby Street.

Back in the kitchen, Gromit sat down at the table and opened the green envelope. It was a birthday card with a picture of a smiling dog on the front, and when he opened it, it played *Happy Birthday to You!*

Gromit put the card on the table and looked at it sadly. Only one birthday card on his birthday!

Just then a red **light** over his head began to go on and off.

Upstairs Wallace was in bed. There was a red **button** next to his bed. It said *Breakfast* on it. Wallace hit it again and again. *Breakfast* said the red light in the kitchen over Gromit's head.

envelope a paper cover that you put on a letter

toy something that a child plays with

shoot (*past* **shot**) to move quickly, or to use a gun

machine something that does work for people

light something that you can see which tells you when a machine is working

button a small round thing that you push to make a machine work

Down in the kitchen Gromit moved a **lever** behind his chair. At once, up in Wallace's room, the head of the bed moved up. At the same time a door opened in the **floor** at the foot of the bed. The table in the kitchen was right under this door. Suddenly Wallace shot out of bed, crying 'Gromit!' He shot down through the door in the floor, and was soon downstairs, sitting in his chair at the kitchen table.

'Well Gromit, my *Getting Up in the Morning Machine* worked well,' said Wallace, and he began to eat his breakfast. 'But perhaps I can make it work better. I hit the chair very fast that time. **Cracking** breakfast, Gromit!' he went on.

Gromit read his **newspaper** and said nothing.

'Any letters today?' asked Wallace. Gromit gave him his letters.

Wallace opened the first brown envelope and took out a very long letter asking him for lots of money.

'Oh dear!' said Wallace, looking at the long letter carefully. He looked at all the brown envelopes in his hand. 'We must be more careful with money, Gromit!'

Gromit put his birthday card on the table. It played *Happy Birthday* slowly and sadly, but Wallace wasn't interested in birthday cards just then.

Wallace went to look in his money box. There was only thirty pence in it.

lever a long thing that you move to make a machine work

floor the place in a room where you stand or walk

cracking very good

newspaper people read about new things that happen every day in this

present something that you give to someone on their birthday

chuck my friend

collar something that a dog wears round its neck

lead a person takes one end of this in their hand, the other end goes on a dog's collar

'Look at that!' he said. 'And those **presents** weren't cheap.' He put his hand over his mouth and looked at Gromit. Oh no! He didn't want Gromit to know about his presents just then.

Gromit looked at Wallace, and his ears went up excitedly. 'Perhaps I'm going to get something more for my birthday,' he thought.

'Well, Gromit. What's on the 9.05 train?' said Wallace. 'Oh look! Here it comes now!'

Wallace's little toy train came through the kitchen door and shot past the table. Quickly Wallace took a little present off it. 'What's this?' he said and he put the present on the table in front of Gromit. 'Happy birthday, **chuck**!'

Gromit quickly opened his birthday present. It was a red dog **collar** and **lead**.

'You wanted a collar!' said Wallace, laughing. 'Here, let's put it on you.'

Wallace helped Gromit to put on his collar.

'Now people can see you come from a good home,' he said, 'But that isn't all. Come and look in here.'

Gromit went into the front room. Something stood there in the dark. A new machine perhaps? It began to make a noise and it came out from behind the door. It was a big, walking, present! It walked nearer and nearer to Gromit on its two big legs. Gromit felt very afraid.

Suddenly the thing stopped and Gromit saw a small card on the front of it: *To Gromit, love Wallace* said the card.

Because Gromit was afraid, in the end Wallace opened this second present. But what was it? Green and black trousers!? Yes. But they were trousers with blue buttons and red levers.

'They're **Techno-**trousers!' said Wallace.

techno- to do with machines

READING CHECK

Are these sentences true or false? Tick the boxes.

		True	False
a	Wednesday 12th is Wallace's birthday.	☐	☑
b	Wallace and Gromit live in a house in West Wallaby Street.	☐	☐
c	The postman brings six birthday cards.	☐	☐
d	There are a lot of machines in Wallace and Gromit's house.	☐	☐
e	Wallace gets out of bed and goes downstairs slowly.	☐	☐
f	Wallace gets some letters asking for money.	☐	☐
g	Gromit gets three presents from Wallace.	☐	☐

WORD WORK

1 Find the words in Gromit's pen to complete the sentences.

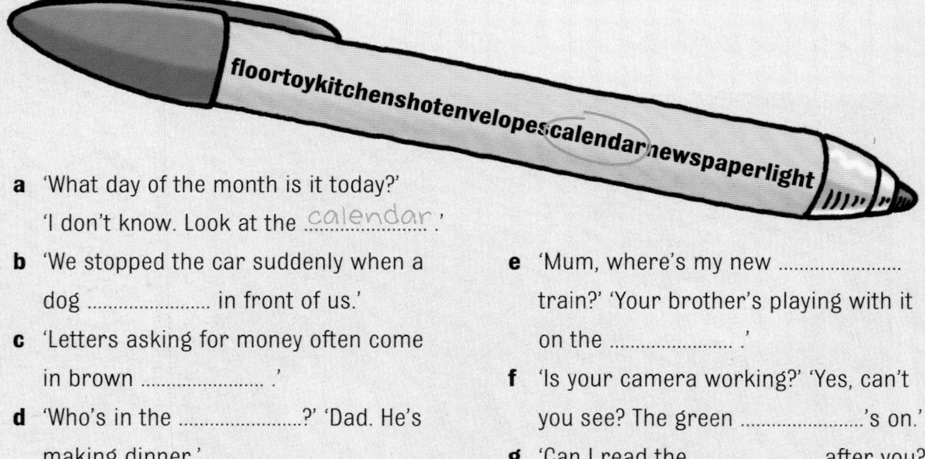

a 'What day of the month is it today?' 'I don't know. Look at the calendar.'

b 'We stopped the car suddenly when a dog .... in front of us.'

c 'Letters asking for money often come in brown ....'

d 'Who's in the ....?' 'Dad. He's making dinner.'

e 'Mum, where's my new .... train?' 'Your brother's playing with it on the ....'

f 'Is your camera working?' 'Yes, can't you see? The green ....'s on.'

g 'Can I read the .... after you?'

2 Find six more words from Chapter 1 in Gromit's collar.

3 Match the words in Activity 2 with the pictures.

a present

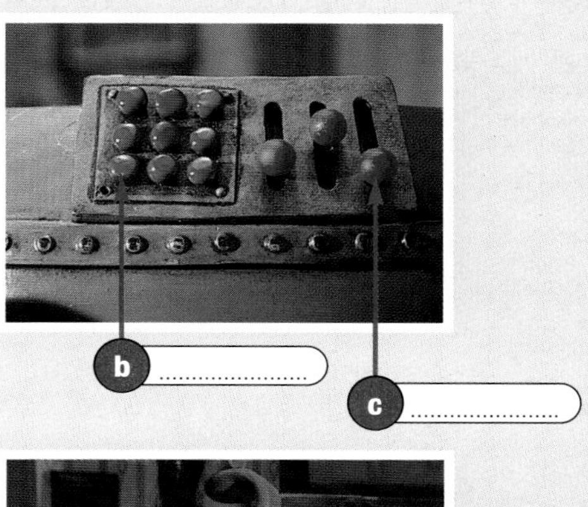

b ....

c ....

d ....

e ....

f ....

GUESS WHAT

What happens in the next chapter? Tick the boxes.

a The Techno-trousers take Gromit . . .

1 ☐ for a walk in the park.

2 ☐ to hospital.

3 ☐ to the shops.

b A new . . . comes to live in West Wallaby Street.

1 ☐ man

2 ☐ woman

3 ☐ animal

c This newcomer wants to live in . . .

1 ☐ Wallace's room.

2 ☐ Gromit's room.

3 ☐ the old room upstairs.

d Gromit makes the old room upstairs look nice with the help of . . .

1 ☐ the Techno-trousers.

2 ☐ his friend Wallace.

3 ☐ the newcomer.

2

Room for rent

other different

sign writing in a place that tells people about something important

park a big garden that is open to everybody to visit

'I think you're going to like these Techno-trousers!' Wallace said. He put one end of Gromit's new lead on his collar and the **other** end on the trousers. Then he hit some blue buttons and moved some red levers.

'Time for a walk. Ten . . . no . . . twenty minutes,' he said.

'Now what's happening?' thought Gromit.

Suddenly the Techno-trousers began walking out of the door and Gromit, in his collar and lead, went sadly with them.

'Have a nice walk Gromit!' Wallace laughed.

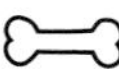

There was a **sign** in the **park**. *ALL DOGS ON A LEAD*, it said. But when Gromit arrived, he didn't have his new lead on. Where was it? On a toy dog! So in the end Gromit played happily in the park and the Techno-trousers took the toy dog for a walk.

At home in 62 West Wallaby Street, Wallace sat in the kitchen. He had all the letters asking for money on the table in front of him.

'It's no good. We need some more money!' he said.

He wrote out a sign and put it in the front window of the house. ***SPARE ROOM*** *FOR* ***RENT***, it said.

Gromit saw the sign when he came back from the park.

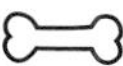

Later that day Wallace and Gromit sat in the front room.

'Did you have a nice walk, chuck?' asked Wallace. 'How were the Techno-trousers?'

Gromit looked at him sadly and said nothing.

Suddenly they heard a **ring** at the front door.

'There's someone at the door, Gromit!'

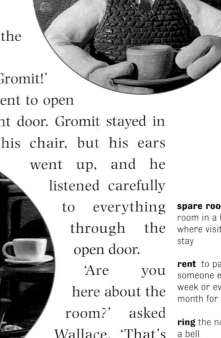

Wallace quickly got up and went to open the front door. Gromit stayed in his chair, but his ears went up, and he listened carefully to everything through the open door.

'Are you here about the room?' asked Wallace. 'That's **grand**! Come in.'

spare room a room in a house where visitors stay

rent to pay someone every week or every month for a room

ring the noise of a bell

grand very good

The next minute a **penguin** walked quietly into 62 West Wallaby Street with a little black bag. He went upstairs with Wallace.

'I'm asking twenty pounds a week. That's with breakfast,' Wallace said to the penguin. They walked past Gromit's room.

'It's cheap because it's a dark room,' said Wallace, opening the door to the spare room. 'But we can soon make it nice.'

The penguin took one look at the dark and dirty spare room and ran into Gromit's room.

'No! Wait a minute!' said Wallace. 'You can't . . .'

But the penguin got up on Gromit's bed, opened his bag, sat back happily and began listening to the radio.

'Yes . . . well . . . that's OK then,' said Wallace slowly, and he left the penguin in Gromit's room, closed the door, and went downstairs.

penguin a black and white bird that cannot fly

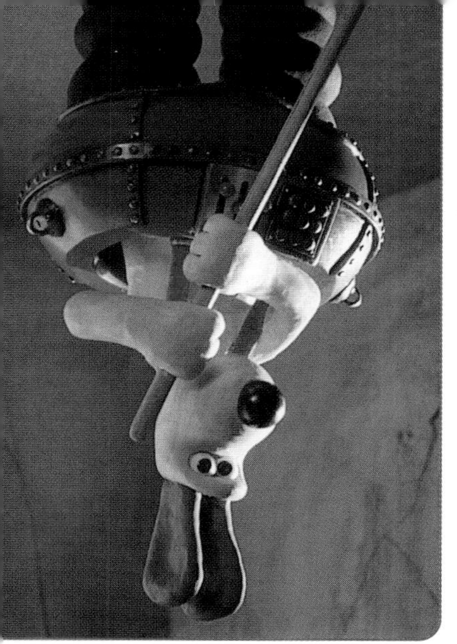

With the penguin now in Gromit's room, Gromit moved into the spare room.

knock to hit strongly

'It's OK, Gromit. We can soon make it nice,' said Wallace.

Of course they had the Techno-trousers to help them. The penguin was very, very interested in those when he saw them.

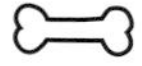

Gromit couldn't sleep in his bed in the spare room that night because he could hear the penguin's radio. He went downstairs, but he could hear the radio there too. Angrily he went upstairs again to speak to the penguin, but he couldn't open the door to his room, and there was no answer when he **knocked** on it.

In the end Gromit went out sadly into the garden, but he could hear the radio out there too. Very late that night, the penguin arrived home. He went into the house, up to his room and to bed. Then the radio stopped and everything went quiet.

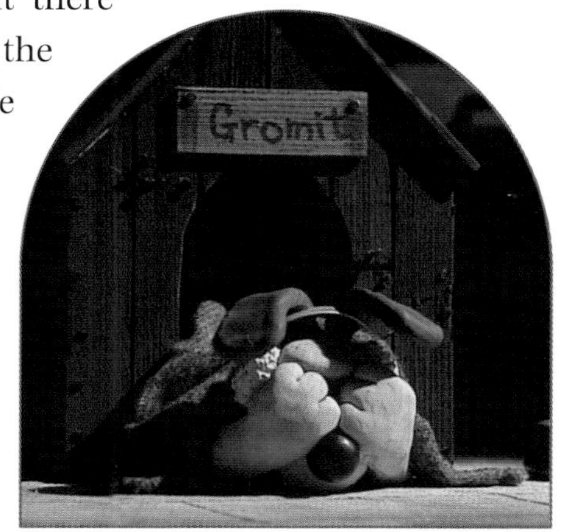

In the garden Gromit put his head in his hands and cried quietly.

READING CHECK

1 Write the sentences.

a Wallace looks at lots of  asking for .

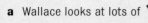

Wallace looks at lots of letters asking for money.

b Gromit goes for a walk with the Techno-trousers in the .

....

c A penguin arrives at the front .

....

d Gromit moves into a different .

....

e Wallace puts the  on Gromit.

....

f Gromit can't sleep because he can hear the penguin's .

....

g The penguin takes his  into Gromit's room and gets on the 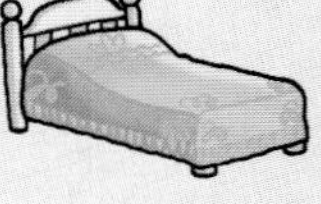.

....

2 Put the sentences in Activity 1 in the correct order. Number them 1-7.

a ☐ **b** ☐ **c** ☐ **d** ☐ **e** 1 **f** ☐ **g** ☐

WORD WORK

Find words in the money to complete the sentences.

a P _ _ _ _ _ _ _ are black and white. They live in and near Antarctica.

b There were lots of s _ _ _ _ with *NO SMOKING* on them in the plane.

c Is the telephone r _ _ _ _ _ _?

d This isn't my car. I'm r _ _ _ _ _ _ it.

e Every day I go running in the p _ _ _ .

f We don't use our s _ _ _ _ r _ _ _ a lot. Only when friends visit us.

g Who is k _ _ _ _ _ _ _ at the front door?

GUESS WHAT

What happens in the next chapter? Tick four sentences.

a ☐ The penguin is very nice to Wallace.
b ☐ Wallace is happy with the penguin.
c ☐ Gromit kills the penguin.
d ☐ Gromit leaves home.
e ☐ The penguin makes the Techno-trousers go wrong.
f ☐ The penguin buys 62 West Wallaby Street.

3

Penguin, that's grand!

The next day, when Gromit went to the **bathroom**, there was someone in there. Gromit waited.

Wallace walked past. 'Good morning, Gromit!' he said happily, and he went down to breakfast.

Then the penguin came out of the bathroom.

Later when Gromit sat down for breakfast, Wallace put his feet up. The penguin quickly brought his **slippers** to him.

'Thank you very much, penguin. That's grand!' said Wallace, putting his feet into the slippers.

Gromit usually took Wallace his newspaper when it came in the morning; but now the penguin got to the front door and back with the newspaper before Gromit.

'What do you think of that, Gromit?' asked Wallace. 'Our new friend's a great help!' he laughed.

Gromit looked at Wallace and the penguin and he felt angrier and angrier.

bathroom the room in the house where you wash

slippers shoes that people wear in the house

That evening Gromit went out into the garden again. Through the window he could see Wallace and the penguin eating and drinking happily in the back room.

'More **cheese**, penguin?' asked Wallace.

Gromit looked away sadly. He went into his **kennel**, and put two or three of his most important things into a red and white bag. Before he left, he took an old photo of Wallace in his hands and looked at it for a minute or two. Then he put the photo down, put on his yellow coat and hat, put his bag on his back, and walked off into the rain.

'Goodnight, penguin! Sleep well,' called Wallace.

Under the cold rain Gromit slowly walked away from his kennel, away from his home in West Wallaby Street, and away from his old friend Wallace.

From the house the penguin watched Gromit go, and was happy. Then he went off to find the Techno-trousers.

cheese yellow food that you make from milk

kennel a small house for a dog that you have in your garden

bin a metal box in the street where you put things that you don't want

land to come down to the floor

control panel the part of a machine with the buttons and levers that make it work

The next morning Gromit got up early after a night sleeping in a **bin** in the street. At home, in West Wallaby Street, Wallace was happy in his bed. He opened his eyes slowly.

Just then the head of his bed moved up and the door opened in the floor at the foot of the bed. Wallace shot out of bed, through the door in the floor and down into the kitchen.

But this time he didn't **land** in his usual brown trousers, he landed in the Techno-trousers.

'They're the wrong trousers!' he cried.

Then the trousers moved, but there was no control panel on the front of them to stop them.

'Where's the **control panel**?' cried Wallace. 'Stop them, Gromit! Get me out of these trousers!'

But Gromit wasn't there and the Techno-trousers didn't stop. They walked out of the front door, and down the street with Wallace in them.

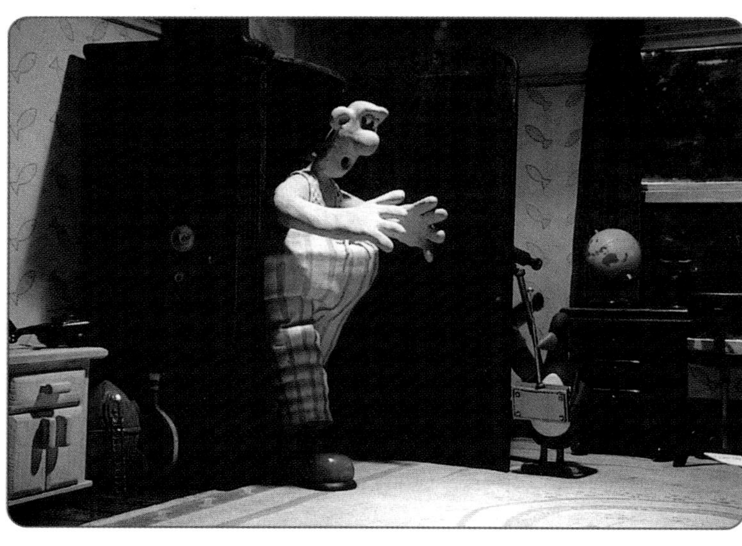

Gromit looked at a sign in a shop window. *SPARE ROOM TO RENT. CHEAP.* it said. 'Oh, good!' he thought. He read more. *NO DOGS!* the sign went on. 'Oh, no!' thought Gromit.

SPARE ROOM
TO RENT
CHEAP
NO DOGS!

Then he saw a picture of a chicken in the window. *Help us to find this* ***chicken****, and you get £1,000,* Gromit read. He looked at the picture carefully. Did he know that chicken's face?

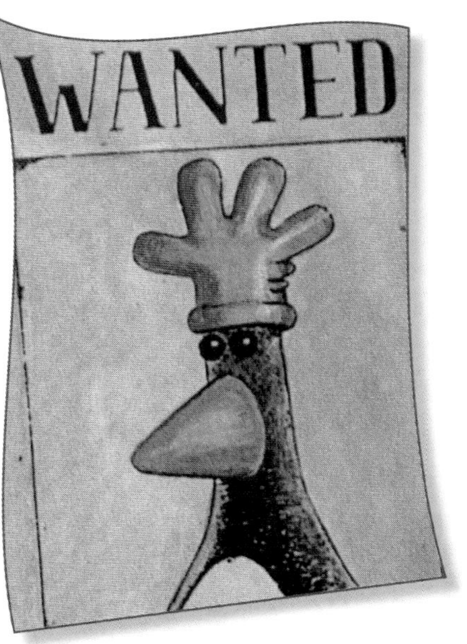

Just then Wallace ran past in the Techno-trousers.

'Help! Gromit!' he cried. 'They're the wrong trousers!'

Gromit ran after his old friend.

'What's wrong with the Techno-trousers?' he thought.

And then, in the street in front of him, he saw the penguin.

'What's he got there?' thought Gromit.

Quietly he moved nearer, and then he saw. The penguin had the control panel! Now Gromit understood. With the buttons and levers the penguin could make the Techno-trousers move here and there, up and down, and Wallace couldn't stop him.

In the end the Techno-trousers took Wallace home. He felt very tired by then. Because he couldn't get out of the Techno-trousers, he went to bed in them. And he went to sleep at once.

chicken a bird that has eggs which people eat

READING CHECK

Complete the sentences with the correct names.

the penguin

Wallace

Gromit

a The penguin .... does lots of little things to help Wallace.
b .... feels angry.
c .... has dinner with the penguin.
d .... puts his things into a bag and leaves home.
e .... takes the control panel off the Techno-trousers.
f .... sleeps in the street.
g .... can't get out of the Techno-trousers.

WORD WORK

Match the words with the correct pictures.

a ~~slippers~~ bathroom ....

b cheese ....

c kennel ....

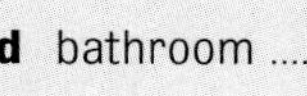

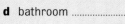

d bathroom ....

e chicken ....

f bin ....

g newspaper ....

h control panel ....

GUESS WHAT

What happens in the next chapter? Match the parts of these sentences.

a Gromit watches . . .
b The penguin goes to look . . .
c The penguin writes lots of . . .
d Gromit goes quickly to . . .
e When the penguin arrives . . .
f Wallace walks down the street . . .

1 without waking up.
2 62 West Wallaby Street.
3 the penguin carefully.
4 Gromit goes into Wallace's room.
5 at an old building.
6 things in a little book.

4

Watching and waiting

hide (*past* **hid**) to go where nobody can see you

hole an opening in something that you can look through

Gromit was in a coffee shop. He looked over his newspaper at the street, and saw the penguin walking past. He quickly put his newspaper down, left some money for his coffee on the table, and went out into the street, after the penguin.

Soon the penguin stopped in front of a big, old, building.

'What's he doing here?' thought Gromit.

Suddenly the penguin looked behind him. Gromit quickly **hid** behind some bins.

Then the penguin looked back at the big, old, building and began writing lots of things down in a little book.

Gromit got under an old box and moved slowly nearer to the old building. But how could he see out now? Easy! He took out a little red knife, made a **hole** in the front of the box, and looked carefully through it.

Now the penguin had a yellow **tape measure** in his hand. First he looked up at a **high** window over his head. After that he made his tape measure very long and put one end of it up on the **ledge** in front of the high window. And then, when the other end of the tape measure went up, the penguin shot up with it and landed on the high window ledge.

Up there on the ledge the penguin looked at the big window in front of him carefully. He **measured** it from left to right and up and down and he wrote lots more things down in his little book.

When he finished writing, he put his book under his arm, and he put one end of the tape measure on the window ledge again. And then, when the other end of the tape measure went down, the penguin came down with it and landed in the street. He began walking past Gromit's box.

Suddenly he stopped and looked right at the box.

'Oh, no! He knows I'm in here,' thought Gromit, and he watched and waited.

But in the end the penguin only looked at the box for a minute and then walked on.

tape measure you can see how long something is with this

high far up from the floor

ledge a long flat stone under a window

measure to see how long something is

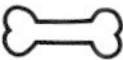

Soon after that, Gromit came out from under the box and ran back to 62 West Wallaby Street. He got there before the penguin and at once went upstairs into his old room, now the penguin's room.

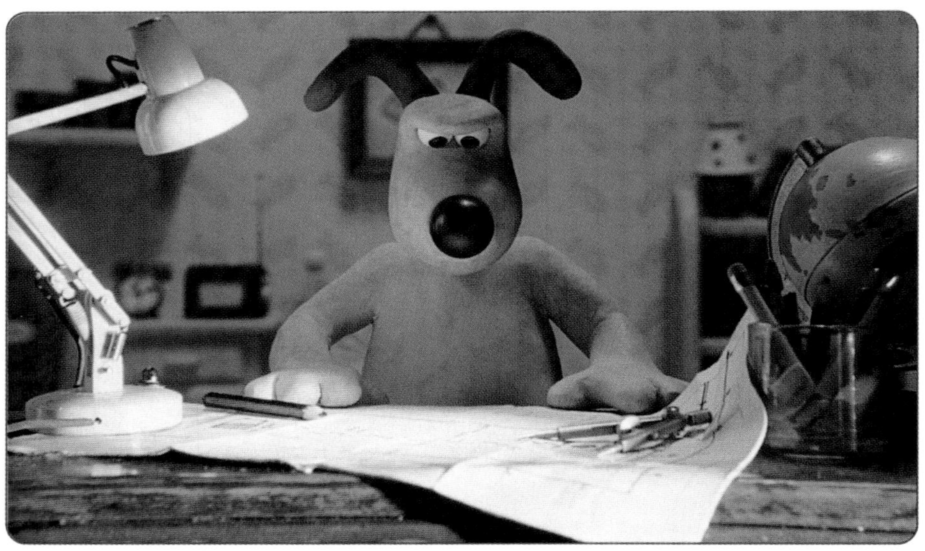

He found something very interesting on the penguin's table. It was a picture of the big, old, building and all the different rooms in it. It was the town **museum**! And there, in the **diamond** room on the second floor, not far from the window, was a big blue diamond.

'Of course!' thought Gromit. 'The penguin wants to get the blue diamond from the museum!'

Just then he heard the back door open and close.

'Oh, no! The penguin's back!' thought Gromit. 'Where can I hide now?'

There was no time to run away. So in the end Gromit hid in bed next to Wallace. When he looked out, he saw the penguin bringing a big box into Wallace's room.

museum a building where people go to look at old things

diamond a very expensive stone that usually has no colour

Then the penguin put the box down, and Gromit saw the red **glove** on his head. At once he remembered the picture of the chicken in the shop window.

'So he's the chicken!' thought Gromit, and he hid again quickly.

Now the penguin took a red **helmet** out of the box and put it on Wallace's head. Wallace slept happily through this.

With the control panel of the Techno-trousers the penguin made Wallace get out of bed, walk downstairs and leave the house. Wallace slept through all this. And the penguin walked down the street after him to the town museum.

At the same time, back in Wallace's room, the *Getting Up Machine* began working. The head of the bed moved up, the door opened in the floor at its foot, and Gromit shot down through it. He landed, in Wallace's brown trousers, at the kitchen table and there he got breakfast all over his face.

glove people usually wear this on their hand

helmet a hard hat that people wear when they are on a bicycle

activities

READING CHECK

Correct these sentences.

a Gromit sees the penguin in the park and goes after him.

b The penguin stops in front of a small old building.

c Gromit is watching him from a bin in the street.

d Gromit gets to 62 West Wallaby Street after the penguin.

e He finds something interesting on the penguin's bed.

f Gromit hides in Wallace's chair when the penguin comes home.

g With the control panel the penguin moves Wallace, and they leave the town.

i Gromit gets breakfast on his feet when the *Getting Up Machine* goes wrong.

WORD WORK

Find words in the tape measure to complete the sentences on page 25.

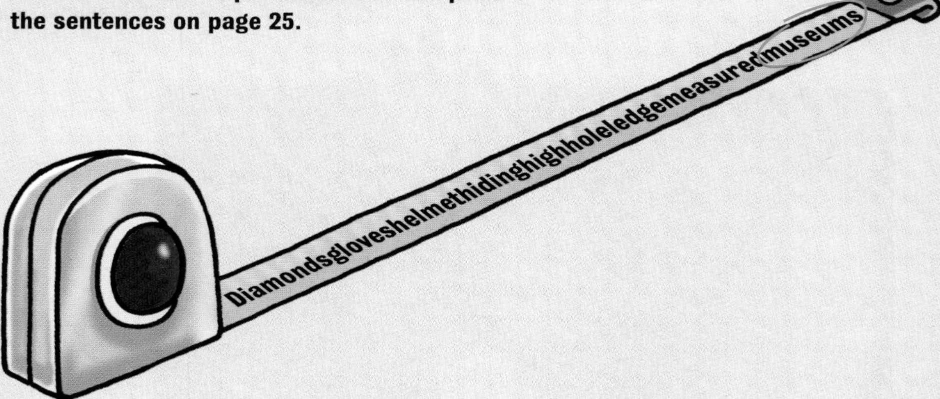

a I like visiting museums and looking at the old things in them.

b When you are on a bicycle you must wear a ....

c In cold weather people wear .... on their hands.

d .... are very expensive.

e I can't find my little sister. Perhaps she is .... from me.

f Look! There's a man standing on that window ....

g Everest is very .... It's 8,848 metres.

h Look through the .... in that box. What can you see?

i My teacher .... me earlier today and I'm taller than all my friends.

GUESS WHAT

What happens in next chapter? Tick the boxes.

a Who goes into the museum?

1 ☐ The penguin.
2 ☐ Gromit.
3 ☐ Wallace.

b What does the penguin do?

1 ☐ He watches through the window.
2 ☐ He listens on the radio.
3 ☐ He waits by the door.

c How does the penguin get the blue diamond?

1 ☐ With Wallace's hand.
2 ☐ With the control panel and the helmet.
3 ☐ With Gromit's help.

d When does Wallace open his eyes?

1 ☐ When he arrives at the museum.
2 ☐ When he leaves the museum.
3 ☐ When he arrives home.

5
Ups and downs

Wallace and the penguin walked through the dark streets to the museum. And Wallace didn't open his eyes once.

When they arrived at the museum, the penguin moved some levers on the control panel. Then he **jumped** up on the Techno-trousers and at once they began to walk up the **wall** of the museum.

Soon the trousers arrived at the high window and here the penguin jumped off and landed on the window ledge.

He looked through the window at the beautiful blue diamond and moved some more levers on the control panel.

The Techno-trousers went higher up the wall with Wallace in them. At last they arrived at the **roof**. There they walked up, over, and down an **air vent**, through the roof and down into the museum. And Wallace slept through it all.

jump to move your feet quickly off the floor and land in a different place

wall a building usually has doors or windows in this

roof the thing on top of a building that stops the rain coming in

air vent a hole in a building for hot air to come out or cold air to come in

Now the penguin could see the Techno-trousers through the window. They came down through an air vent in the ceiling, walked over the ceiling **tiles** in the long room, and came nearer and nearer to the diamond room.

But Wallace had long arms and the penguin suddenly felt afraid. Those long arms could easily get in front of the **alarm** and make it ring. So he stopped the trousers for a time.

In the end Wallace moved his arms in his sleep, and the penguin quickly moved some levers on the control panel and walked him past the alarm. Now the diamond was under him.

Then the penguin hit a button on the control panel and the red helmet on Wallace's head opened and a **steel** machine **claw** came down out of it.

After that the penguin hit a different button and moved some of the levers on the control panel. The trousers moved and the machine claw went down to the diamond and opened over it.

tiles square things that people put all over the ceiling or floor

alarm a bell that rings when someone bad is taking something from a shop or house

steel very strong metal

claw a hand with (usually) three fingers; the hand of an animal

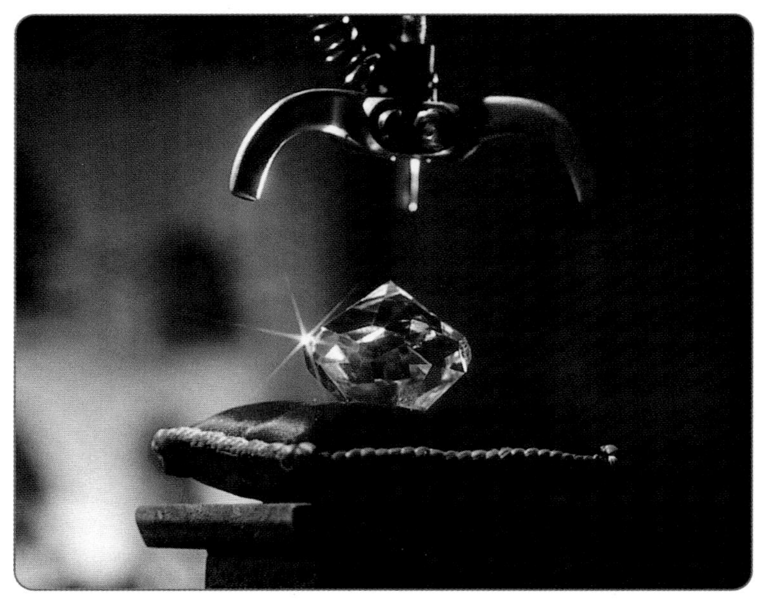

Now the steel claw closed on the diamond and the penguin hit some more buttons. The claw, with the diamond in it, slowly began to go up into Wallace's helmet. Then, suddenly, the diamond shot out of the claw. At once the penguin moved a lever and hit a button. The steel claw shot down and closed on the diamond again before it hit the floor.

Once again the penguin hit some more buttons and the claw moved up into the helmet with the diamond in it.

Then it happened.

One of the ceiling tiles came off the ceiling, and with it came one of the feet of the Techno-trousers. At the same time the helmet opened again and the steel claw with the diamond in moved down in front of the alarm. The alarm began to ring. Lights began to go on and off.

Wallace opened his eyes.

'Where am I? What's that noise?' he cried.

At the same time a big steel door closed in front of him. How could the penguin get the diamond out of the museum now? The air vent was in the long room behind the steel door.

'Gromit! Gromit!' cried Wallace.

The penguin hit some buttons and moved some levers on the control panel. The Techno-trousers walked to the window and stood on it. At once the window opened and Wallace was out in the cold, standing on a high window looking up at the night sky. Now the trousers moved and he could see the dark street under him.

'Get me down!' cried Wallace. 'Help!'

Then the penguin jumped on Wallace's back and the Techno-trousers quickly walked down the wall and ran away.

'You can't do this to me!' cried Wallace. 'Stop it at once! I'm a good man, I am.'

READING CHECK

1 Complete the chapter summary.

Wallace and the penguin **a)** ....walk.... to the museum. The penguin jumps on to the Techno-trousers and then jumps off them onto the ledge under the high **b)** .... Wallace is sleeping in the Techno-trousers. The trousers walk up past the penguin and then down into the museum. They walk into a long room with the **c)** .... diamond in it. Then the penguin hits a **d)** .... on the control panel. Something comes out of the **e)** .... on Wallace's head. It's a machine hand! The hand takes the **f)** .... but suddenly there is a ringing noise and Wallace opens his **g)** .... Steel doors start to **h)** .... and the Techno-trousers, with Wallace in them, leave the museum through the window.

2 Match the words with the things in the town museum.

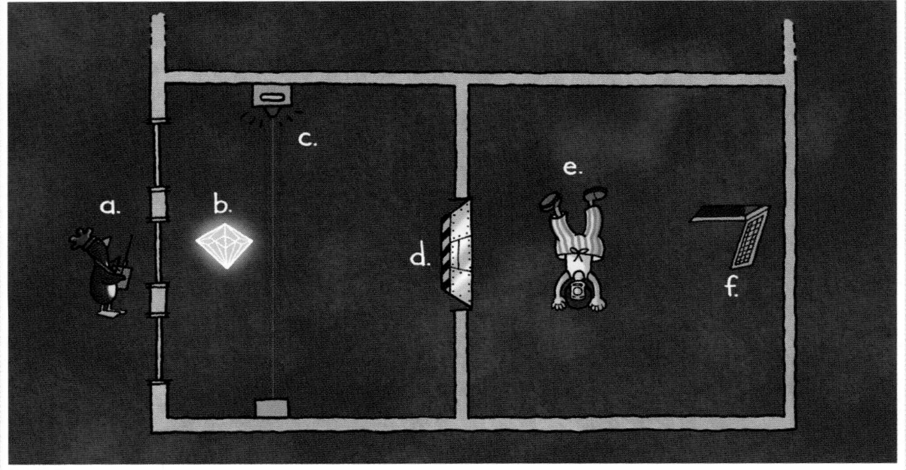

f	air vent	☐	diamond	☐	steel doors
☐	alarm	☐	penguin	☐	techno-trousers

WORD WORK

Use the words in the diamond to complete the sentences.

a The Techno-trousers get into the museum through the air vent.

b There's a hole in the _ _ _ _ of our house. When it rains, water comes in through it.

c You can't break a _ _ _ _ _ door very easily.

d Our car has got an _ _ _ _ _ in it to stop people from taking it.

e Can you _ _ _ _ from this tree to that tree?

f We have got blue _ _ _ _ _ on the _ _ _ _ _ in our bathroom.

g The cat had something in its _ _ _ _ _ .

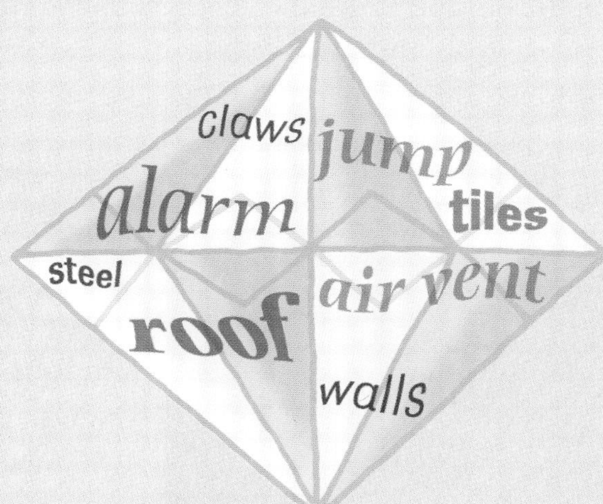

GUESS WHAT

What happens in the next chapter? Tick the boxes.	**Yes**	**Perhaps**	**No**
a The penguin and Wallace go to West Wallaby Street.	☐	☐	☐
b Wallace takes the diamond.	☐	☐	☐
c Gromit runs after the penguin.	☐	☐	☐
d The penguin leaves the country.	☐	☐	☐
e Wallace and Gromit get the penguin.	☐	☐	☐
f Wallace and Gromit get a thousand pounds.	☐	☐	☐
g The Techno-trousers stay at West Wallaby Street.	☐	☐	☐

6

Be careful, lad!

The penguin took Wallace back to his room at 62 West Wallaby Street. There, Wallace took off the helmet and put it down. There, too, the penguin took the red glove off his head.

'Oh! It's *you*!' said Wallace, for he saw now it wasn't a chicken standing in front of him, but the penguin. Then he got angry. 'Get me out of these trousers this minute,' he said.

wardrobe a big piece of furniture where you put things to wear

rolling pin you use this in the kitchen to make things flat

gun people fight with these

In answer the penguin quickly put Wallace into a **wardrobe**, and closed the door behind him.

'Help! Open this door at once!' cried Wallace in the wardrobe, and he knocked on the door angrily.

The penguin took the diamond from the helmet and put it in a bag. Then he walked to the door.

But Gromit stood at the door. He was angry and he had a big **rolling pin** in his hands.

At once the penguin took out a big black **gun**. When he saw that, Gromit put his rolling pin down. Now the penguin opened the wardrobe door, Gromit got in with Wallace, and the penguin closed the door again.

In the dark Gromit began to put his hands down the front of the Techno-trousers.

'What are you doing?' cried Wallace, 'Be careful, **lad**!'

Gromit put the end of a red **wire** on the end of a black wire and the legs of the Techno-trousers began to move up and down, faster and faster. Soon the wardrobe broke away from the floor and the trousers walked it out of the room with Wallace and Gromit in it.

'Where are we going? I can't see a thing!' cried Wallace. Then the wardrobe door opened and Gromit came out.

The penguin jumped on the **banister** and went down it with the gun in his hand, and the diamond bag on his back. He landed on the front of Wallace's toy train.

'Get him, Gromit!' cried Wallace from in the wardrobe.

Then the wardrobe began to go downstairs with Wallace in it. Gromit jumped up at once and caught the ceiling lamp. The penguin shot the lamp down from the ceiling and Gromit landed near the back of Wallace's toy train with the lamp on his head. The train went off quickly down the track.

lad young man

wire a long, very thin, metal thing in a machine

banister you put your hand on this when you go upstairs or downstairs

engine the machine at the front of a train which makes it move

lamp you have this in a house to help you see at night

catch (*past* **caught**) to take quickly in your hands

track the road which a train moves on

The penguin was now behind the little blue train **engine**. He looked back and shot at Gromit again and again with his gun.

But Gromit wasn't afraid. He had a **lamp** for a helmet on his head, and he wanted to **catch** the penguin.

Suddenly he saw the train getting near the back door.

'Oh no! The penguin's going to get away!' he thought. He hit a red button by the **track** and the train went off to the left.

'It's OK Gromit,' cried Wallace. He now stood on the last car at the end of the train on one leg of the Techno-trousers. 'I'm behind you, lad!' he called.

Now the penguin shot his gun at Wallace's feet and Wallace's car jumped off the track and began to run on a new track next to the first.

'Stay there, Gromit! Everything's OK.' called Wallace.

And he moved past his friend and got near the penguin.

'Give me that gun!' cried Wallace.

He put out his hand and took the gun from the penguin, but suddenly the Techno-trousers hit the wall and Wallace came out of them, went through a hole in the wall, and landed on a kitchen **trolley**. At once Gromit took the lamp off his head and began to move to the front of the train. Wallace went past him again. This time he was on his trolley, and he had a **net** in his hands.

'I'm going to get that penguin now!' he cried.

But then Wallace's net hit something on the wall and this knocked him off the trolley. He landed back on the train. The penguin hit a little lever by the track. The engine, with the penguin on a car behind it, went off along one track. The back of the train, with Gromit on the first car and Wallace on the last car, went off along a different track.

trolley a table with wheels on that you can move easily

net you catch things in this

Suddenly Gromit had no more track in front of him.

'Oh no! We're going to have an accident!' he thought.

Then he saw a box of new track on the floor, caught it, and quickly began to put the new track down in front of the train. So they went on, under the table, and into the next room.

There Gromit's track ran over the penguin's track. At the back of the train Wallace put out his hands to catch the penguin, but he only caught the little blue toy engine.

Then the Techno-trousers walked in front of the penguin's car, and the penguin – with the diamond bag on his back – **flew** up off the car and into the kitchen.

At the same time Gromit hit the kitchen **cupboard**, and stopped suddenly. A milk bottle came down off the cupboard and landed in his hand. A second later the penguin landed in the milk bottle and the diamond bag landed in Gromit's other hand.

'We did it, Gromit, lad! We caught him!' cried Wallace.

fly (*past* **flew**) to go through the air

cupboard you put things in this

That afternoon they took the penguin to the **police** and the police put him away in a very strong building for a very long time.

That evening Wallace and Gromit sat in the front room. They were friends again.

'Now we've got the thousand pounds from the police, we don't need to rent that spare room. Isn't that grand?' said Wallace happily. 'Shall we have some cheese, chuck?'

When Gromit got up to get the cheese, he looked out of the window at the old Techno-trousers, now in a bin in the street. 'And we don't need *you!*' he thought happily. He went back into the front room with Wallace's cheese and then sat down to read the newspaper.

Out in the street, with no control panel to stop them, the Techno-trousers got up and walked off into the night.

police they find people who do something bad

READING CHECK

Match the first and second parts of the sentences.

a	The penguin takes Wallace . . .	**1**	off his head.
b	There the penguin takes the glove . . .	**2**	in a bag.
c	Wallace says . . .	**3**	'It's you!' to the penguin.
d	The penguin puts the diamond . . .	**4**	to West Wallaby Street.
e	Gromit jumps on the back of the train . . .	**5**	leave 62 West Wallaby Street.
f	After some time Wallace and Gromit . . .	**6**	for catching the penguin.
g	They get £1,000 . . .	**7**	and moves to the front of it.
h	In the end The Techno-trousers . . .	**8**	catch the penguin.

WORD WORK

1 Correct the mistakes in these sentences. The words you need are all in Chapter 6.

a Oh no! He's got a **sun** and he's going to kill someone with it. ...gun...

b I'm not good at football or tennis. I can't **watch** things in my hands very well. ....

c Trains travel on **truck.** ....

d My radio has lots of different coloured **wives** in it. ....

e I can catch things with my **not.** ....

f I have a **lump** by my bed so I can read at night. ....

2 Find five more words from Chapter 6 in the cheese.

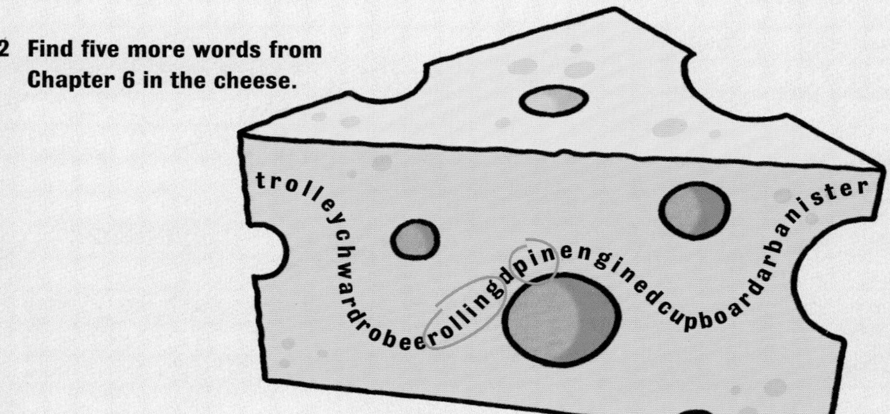

3 There are seven more letters in the picture. Write them in order to find the name of a famous English cheese. c _ _ _ _ _ _

4 Match the words in Activity 2 with the pictures.

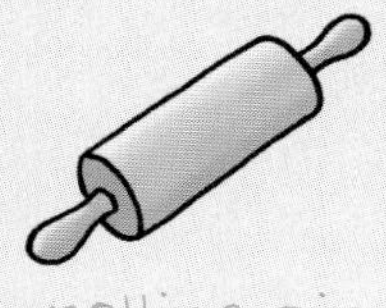

a rolling pin

b ....

c ....

d ....

e ....

f ....

GUESS WHAT

What happens after the story finishes? Choose from these ideas or add your own.

a ☐ Wallace and Gromit go on holiday.

b ☐ Wallace buys Gromit some new Techno-trousers.

c ☐ Wallace and Gromit start cleaning windows.

d ☐ Wallace meets a beautiful woman and forgets Gromit.

e ☐ Gromit meets a beautiful girl dog and forgets Wallace.

PROJECT A A Dictionary of Informal English

1 Write these words from *The Wrong Trousers* in the correct places in the *Dictionary of Informal English*.

lad chuck cracking grand

WORD	MEANING	EXAMPLE SENTENCE
a	very good	This is a .... breakfast.
b	very good	Penguin, that's ....
c	a name for someone that you like	Happy birthday, ...!
d	young man	Be careful, ...

2 Can you translate the words in Activity 1 into informal words in your language?

3 Match these words and the underlined words in the sentences on page 41. Use a dictionary to help you.

a Let's meet later. I'll call you on the telephone that I carry with me about 8 o'clock.

b I'm fat because I eat a lot of food.

c My stomach hurts.

d I like sausages a lot.

e What a nice shirt!

f The new girl in our class is strange.

g Where's the nearest toilet?

4 Make a dictionary for the words in Activity 3 (or some other informal words). After each word write these things.

a a formal English word that means the same (a synonym), or a definition of the word

b an example sentence and a translation

WORD	SYNONYM / DEFINITION	EXAMPLE SENTENCE / TRANSLATION

PROJECT B *A new invention*

1 Match the words with the picture of the 'Techno-trousers'. Use a dictionary to help you.

Why not buy a pair of . . .
TECHNO-TROUSERS?
NEW
1
2
3
4
5
Why not buy a pair of new Techno-trousers? These are the latest invention from NASA (The North American Space Agency). With their sticky feet, rubber legs, and built-in control panel, they are perfect for walking the dog, painting walls and ceilings and many other things.
Quality
For people with a MODERN lifestyle.

a ☐ sticky feet can walk up walls or across ceiling

b ☐ hit the blue buttons and move the red levers on the control panel to program the trousers

c ☐ rubber legs move up and down and to front and back

d ☐ you can get into the trousers here

e ☐ you can put a dog's lead through here

Why not buy a new . . .
Sun and Rain Suit
1
2
3
4
5
new
Why not buy a new .... and .... suit? This is the latest invention from AWS (All Weather Suits). With its brightly-coloured sun and rain .... for your head, its .... and its ...., it is perfect for sunny days. It has a .... and .... for rainy days too! And the .... helps you to get ready for good or bad weather!
Another AWS invention!

2 Look at this 'Sun and Rain Suit'. Match the words with the picture.

- **a** ☐ sun and rain umbrella
- **b** ☐ sun-cream to put on your face on sunny days
- **c** ☐ sunglasses to put in front of your eyes on sunny days
- **d** ☐ raincoat and rainshoes for rainy days
- **e** ☐ weather house to see the weather before it happens

3 Complete the advertisement.

4 **Choose one these inventions (or invent something new and different). Explain how your invention works, and write an advertisement for it.**

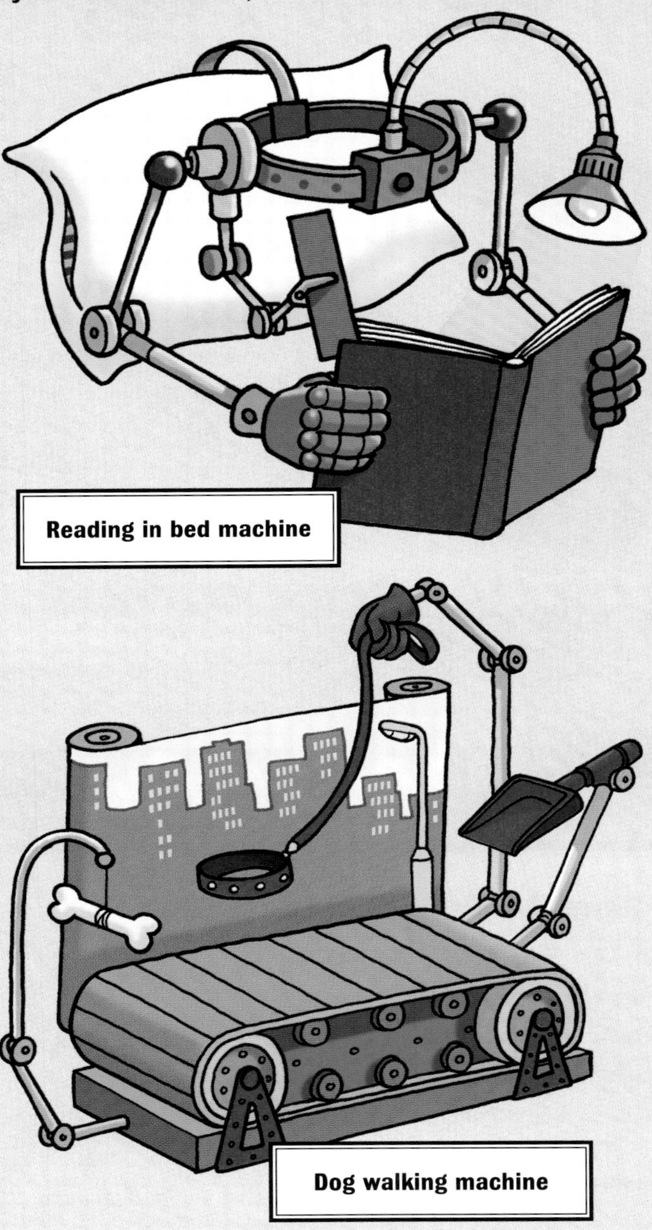